T0208749

HELP!
In Perilous Times

BISHOP HATTIE DANCIL-SMALL

authorHOUSE®

AuthorHouse™
1663 Liberty Drive
Bloomington, IN 47403
www.authorhouse.com
Phone: 1 (800) 839-8640

Published by AuthorHouse 06/23/2020

ISBN: 978-1-7283-6476-6 (sc)
ISBN: 978-1-7283-6475-9 (e)

Library of Congress Control Number: 2020911064

Print information available on the last page.

CONTENTS

FORWARD

I have known Bishop Hattie Dancil-Small for a very long time and continue to interact with her on many levels. I interact with her as a dear friend; as a fellow Pastor having a passion for the evangelization of our city; as a student at PCIM Bible College and Seminary as one of our very first graduates, one who graduated with honors; and finally as a mentor.

It comes as no surprise to me that Bishop Dancil-Small would undertake to write this book entitled: *Help in Perilous Times*. I say this because being an encourager comes supernaturally natural for her. This is who she is at the very core of her being--to constantly encourage those around her, offer hope, empower, and uplift everyone. This is what you will find in the pages of her new book.

Perilous times are times of great risks, great dangers; times that are hazardous. Dear friends, these words precisely describe the times we are living in at this moment. The population at large is beside itself with fear, anxiety, and frustration. Even the members of the body of Christ find themselves in the same mode of life as the people outside the body of Christ. Almost everyone is hesitant to venture out of their places of quarantine because of the risks of potentially being exposed to the dangerous coronavirus. But there is help, and there is hope, and there is encouragement!

That is what Bishop Dancil-Small brings to you in the pages of this phenomenal book. As you dive into this book, you will come away strengthened, encouraged, hopeful and ready to take life by the tail; you will realize that God sees the great value that He has placed in you and will never leave you as He has promised. You will be empowered with the knowledge that with God on your side, no matter how perilous the times are, there is help for you in our great God. "Preach the word of God. Be prepared, whether the time is favorable or not. Patiently correct, rebuke, and encourage your people with good teaching." (2 Timothy 4:2 NLT2)

Dr. Pat Clarke, Apostle

President- Pat Clarke International Ministries, Inc.

PCIM Bible College and Seminary

Senior Pastor - Faith Connection International Church.

ACKNOWLEDGEMENTS

I give thanks to God for his direction, protection, and the ability to write this book. I want to express my deepest thanks and appreciation to Kingdom Harvest Outreach Ministry where I serve as Senior Pastor. I acknowledge your continued encouragement and your faith in me as I serve as your spiritual leader. I'm thankful to Dr. Pat Clarke for being my mentor and friend and for contributing the forward to this book. I'm thankful for the Sounds of Praise Pentecostal Fellowship Ministry, Inc. You have supported me greatly and you have always been there for me since I said "yes" to serve in ministry.

I'm thankful for my students in both middle and high school, who encouraged me to write a book many years ago. I am known for being one who will encourage others to be the absolute best they can be, but in this instance, they were the ones encouraging me. A special "thank you" to all of my family for your support. It was my mom, Ida Williams Stokes who instilled in me the belief that I could anything I wanted to do and that all things are possible if I believe in God and in myself.

I am so incredibly grateful to my caring, loving, and supportive husband, Deacon Donnie Small. Your encouragement and love for me is duly noted.

May the Almighty God bless each of you.

INTRODUCTION

While writing this book, I found my voice. I found something new inside of me. I found the freedom to speak, express, and to let myself be heard. As a pastor this should have been easy for me to do. But I often times struggled with being confident and a feeling of self-assurance that all things were possible for me to accomplish. I questioned my ability even though I taught others how to trust themselves to walk in the self-confidence.

This book is being written during an exceedingly difficult time in the world. It is during the terrifying times of the COVID-19 virus, an infectious, acute, and deadly disease. It had spread globally, resulting in the coronavirus pandemic. To help stop the spread of the virus, many were asked to stay at home and shelter in place away from others. Businesses were closed. Schools were closed.

Many were laid off of their jobs. The stock markets were in decline and millions of people, the most in decades, were unemployed. It was a critical and devastating time like none have ever seen. Thousands died and thousands more that tested positive for the virus were quarantined. Many walked in fear of this invisible virus not knowing where it would hit next. I found myself seeking the Lord and His word. I was encouraged when he said in Isaiah 43:2 KJV: "When thou passest through the waters, I will be with thee; and through the rivers, they shall not overflow thee: when thou walkest through the fire, thou shalt not be burned; neither shall the flame kindle upon thee". What God is saying to us is that no matter the condition we find ourselves in, he will be with us. He promised to always be with us in the worst of situations.

During these dark days, I found myself preaching messages to encourage and inspire the church. The people needed hope and something to hold on to. Thus, the title of this book, **Help! In Perilous Times**. Paul writes in 2 Timothy 3:1 KJV "This know also, that in the last days perilous times shall come". The word perilous means dangerous, grave, serious, threatening, and unhealthy (Webster). Some of you may describe these as the worst of times. But as you look back over your lives, you could say that there were times, other than this virus, that you found yourself in peril. Some have encountered the loss a dear loved one and are unable to be comforted. Others have endured the death of a marriage and are unable to move forward, always dwelling in the past. Others have lost their children to the jails and prisons which keeps them bound and imprisoned not only physically but mentally. Some have been diagnosed with serious and deadly diseases with no hope of a cure. Perilous, serious, deadly times. But, no matter how grave the situations and circumstances are in your life, there is hope. This book is not about how bad things are or could be, but to encourage you to not give up and to keep standing strong.

The Holy Spirit gave me the title, Help!! in Perilous Times. Many were in despair during the COVID-19 virus. Those that were laid off of their jobs did not know how they were going to feed their families or pay their bills. They found themselves in a wave of despair. Many people did not know who or where to go to for help. My advice to them on where to go was found in Psalms 121 KJV which tells us that in such times, we are to "look to the hills from whence cometh our help; for our help cometh from the Lord". When others were turning to the news, to local, state, and federal governments, the medical profession, and scientists, I found myself turning to the word of God. Everyone was asking how much longer? No one knew when it would end. Only God knows, for He alone is our help during this perilous time.

I am reminded of Peter walking on the water. Matthew 14:22-36 (KJV) records this story: "And when the disciples saw him (Jesus) walking on the sea, they were all troubled saying, it is a spirit; and they cried out for fear. But Jesus spoke to them, be of good cheer; it is I; be not afraid. And Peter answered him and said, Lord, if it be, thou, bid me come unto thee on the water. And Jesus said, Come. And when Peter was come down out of the ship, he walked on the water, to go to Jesus. But when he saw the wind boisterous, he was afraid; and beginning to sink, he cried saying, Help Lord, save me".

Peter took his eyes off of Jesus and instead began to look upon the boisterous waves around him and became afraid. As he began to sink, he cried out to Jesus to help him. Isn't that what we are asking God to do in this turbulent time, Lord, help, save us!

There are times when many feels like they just could not take another day of sorrow; times when some wanted to throw in the towel. Those who felt like all hope was gone. These messages are meant to encourage you to keep pushing forward. and to just hold on to the promises of God. I believe that this book will revive you and get you back to your purpose. It's a book that was ordained by God to remind us that we are not alone.

CHAPTER 1

More Than A Conqueror

This is your winning season! No matter what is going on around you or in the world, you will come out a winner. During this Corona virus or any other challenging times, God let me know that we will come out better than when we went in. That means you will not lose anything God has for you. The Apostle Paul wrote of overcoming in Romans 8:35–37 NIV, "Who shall separate us from the love of Christ? Shall trouble or hardship or persecution or famine or nakedness or danger or sword? As it is written: "For your sake we face death all day long; we are considered as sheep to be slaughtered." No, in all these things we are more than conquerors through him who loved us". This lets us know that we can live victoriously through Christ who loved us. This does not mean that we will not have problems and trials in our lives. We will. Everything will not go according to your plan. Problems will arise. Circumstances beyond our control will come up. However, we can live above these adversities and be at peace with ourselves and with God. We will have ups and downs seasons in our lives, but we will survive and come out a winner, every time.

When God has selected you, it doesn't matter who else has rejected you. God's favor outweighs all opposition. You are a winner. Without a doubt, with the Lord on your side, you will overcome every adversary. No matter the situations or circumstances of life that you may be going through, it is working for your good even in times of pain and suffering. A conqueror is defined "as a person who gains something by force" (Webster). Sometimes, you have to go into the enemy's camp and take back by force what was taken from you. You can do this because you know you are not alone. You've got the Lord on your side and who will fight for you. Therefore, you cannot lose. You will win, not just once but every time. So, beginning today, declare and decree: I am a champion. I am victorious. I am a conqueror. I am a winner.

No matter what you are facing in life, remember these two things: God is with you and He is in control. You are part of a winning team, God's team. Being a part of a winning team means that you are walking in victory. Just as with athletics, being a champion means you must be disciplined. You must reinforce the desired behavior of never giving up. To be a champion means that you have to know your team, know your opponent, the devil, and know your position on the team. There are no tryouts to be on this winning team. It's not about who can run the fastest, because the race is not given to the swift. Membership on this team, means that you must be born again. Paul in Romans 10:9 (Berean Literal Bible) tells how to be a part of the winning team when He says, "that if you confess with your mouth, Jesus is Lord, and believe in your heart that God raised Him out from the dead, you will be saved". Jesus now becomes the coach of the team and he will lead you into your winning season.

I don't know anyone who does not like to win. From Little League Baseball to the NFL and every other sport in between, the goal is to be on a winning team. There are some who quit the team before getting to the finish line. Why do they quit? Some feel they don't get the recognition they deserve. Stop seeking attention or a platform. Your gift will make room for you. There are some who compare themselves to others on the team and feel as though others are better than them. I encourage you to be yourself and be the best version of you. Do you! Do what is best for you. When you are yourself that's when you are most confident. Being yourself makes you special. You belong to the Lord, and he created you to be one of a kind. "But now thus saith the Lord that created thee, O Jacob, and he that formed thee, O Israel, Fear not: for I have redeemed thee, I have called thee by thy name; thou art mine" (Isaiah 43:1 KJV).

Learning to be confident is extremely important especially at times when you feel like giving up. Many times, over the years, I started writing this book. I would talk myself out of finishing it.

I had many reasons although looking back, they were not good reasons. I'm not a good enough writer. No one would read my book. This takes too much time. Some of you have not completed what you started. You too, had what you thougth were good enough reasons for not doing what God has assigned to your hands to do, i.e.: start that business; go back to school, change your career; record that song, etc.. It's time for you to do your thing.

On God's Team, you will struggle sometimes. You will make mistakes. But no matter how flawed you may be, if you remain a part of God's team you will win. Regardless of the issues in your life, with God on your side, quitting should never be an option. No matter the disappointments in life, things will turn around in your favor. In order to win, you must stay in the race. Your trials may involve physical suffering, unemployment, children who rebel, turmoil or pain. I assure you that God has everything under control. When God sees that you appreciate your now, he starts to release your next. I encourage you to say each day: I am more than a conqueror. I am on a winning team. I have the victory. That's the attitude God wants us to have. Look in the mirror and declare, "There's a winner in me".

———————————— CHAPTER 2 ————————————

You Are Valuable

In the previous chapter we spoke of being confident. I believe that many people do not feel confident. One reason is because people do feel as if they are valuable. Even after receiving the salvation of Jesus Christ, they still question their value and their worth. It is of the utmost importance that we see our value, not in the house we live, the people around us, the money we have, the job we hold. We must see our value in Jesus Christ. Our value is not based on who we are or what we can do, but on what He can do with and through us. Throughout the Bible we are reminded of God's love for us, and how valuable we are to Him. Sometimes others may make fun of us and hurt us and sometimes we make mistakes and hurt ourselves, but value is not based on the opinion of others, it is based on what God says about us.

Then there are those who think that they are not good enough. Let me start by saying no one is good enough. Not me, not you, not your pastor, or anyone else and never let anyone tell you different. Your value is not based on how good you are. The word value means: a thing that is of great worth (Webster). Everyday start the day by confirming that you are of great worth to the Heavenly

Father. We are valuable because we are a part of His creation. He created us in His likeness and image and said, "It is very good!" We are valuable because He says so! Everything that God created was good and that includes you. He doesn't make junk, something that is old or discarded, that is considered useless or of little value. We are of such great worth that God promises to take good care of us. We are told in Matthew 6:2 NIV, "Look at the birds of the air; they do not sow or reap or store away in barns, and yet your heavenly Father feeds them. Are you not much more valuable than they?

We are so valuable to God that after man fell, He immediately began to execute a plan to redeem us from our sin. It is in Genesis 3:15 KJV that lets us know how valuable we are: We are told that God would send a Messiah from the seed of woman to bruise the head of Satan! God showed how much he loved us in that he sent his only begotten son to redeem us. God's plan for us is eternal life, to be with us forever. Not only does He want us to have an eternal life, but He also wants us to have an abundant life. Jesus says in John 10:10 KJV, "the thief cometh not, but for to steal, and to kill, and to destroy, but I am come that they might have life, and that they might have it more abundantly".

As men and women of God, we must know our value even when others don't. Make sure you don't see yourself through the eyes of those who don't value you. See yourself through the eyes of God. The psalmist says in Psalms 139:14 KJV, "I will praise thee; for I am fearfully and wonderfully made: marvelous are thy works; and that my soul knoweth right well.

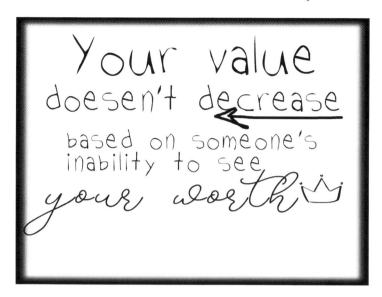

God is saying to each of us, "I want you to live abundantly and eternally with me!" In our Christian walk with God, knowing your worth and value is vital if you're going to have success and happiness in your life. For you to feel fully alive, you must have a strong sense of self-worth and possess confidence. Self-worth is important. It helps us to have better self-esteem. We must know the value of ourselves before we gain the confidence to demonstrate our own value to others. Recognizing our self-worth allows us to believe in ourselves and not let the failures in life and the opinions of others define us.

Your value does not decrease based on someone's inability to see your worth. The more you believe in God, the more you believe in yourself, that all things are possible regardless of the situation you face in life. The more efficient and effective you'll be in all aspects of your life as you keep trusting God. You'll have positive self-esteem, recognize the difference you make, be clear about your values and have a more fulfilling life. That self-worth and confidence comes only in your relationship with the Savior. Everyday remind yourself, "I am valuable!"

‿❧‿

―――――――――― **CHAPTER 3** ――――――――――

Stand firm in the Lord.

To stand firm in the lord means to remain anchored. It is to refuse to change what you have been doing or believing because of all the turmoil surrounding you. Many are in fear and shaken because of what's going on in the world and the effect it is having in their daily lives. He knows everything about you including your pain and suffering and He won't let you be destroyed by it. We are directed in 1 Corinthians 16:13, "Be on your guard; stand firm in the faith; be courageous; be strong (New International Version). I encourage you to stand firm in the Lord and in His word.

No matter what it looks like, no matter what it feels like, everything will work out for your good. Isaiah 41:10 KJV declares, "Fear thou not; for I [am] with thee: be not dismayed; for I [am] thy God: I will strengthen thee; yea, I will help thee; yea, I will uphold thee with the right hand of my righteousness". Even when it looks as though the things God has promised you has been put on hold; He is telling you to stand firm. The same God that delivered us from sin, brought us out of bondage, and healed our bodies before, He is same God who did that and more back then, and He will do it again. For many, this isn't the only virus or calamity that has come our way and it won't be the last. God is telling us in the midst of it all, to stand firm. And while standing in the midst of the storm, continue to stand giving God the praise. We are told in Proverbs 3:3-6 KJV, Let not mercy and truth forsake thee: bind them about thy neck; write them upon the table of thine heart: So shalt thou find favour and good understanding in the sight of God and man. Trust in the LORD with all thine heart; and lean not unto thine own understanding. In all thy ways acknowledge him, and he shall direct thy paths. So give God the praise in advance, knowing that he's directing you to your winning season.

The omnipresent – all knowing, omnipotent – all powerful, and omniscience all seeing God, will bring you out of these perilous times and any other storms in your life. From the time you accepted Christ as your Savior, the Lord God, has made promises to you. God's promises are sure and full of hope. The promises of God are not "yes" then "no". They're not "I don't know" or "maybe so". The promises of God are "Yes!" He will save you. "Yes!" He will heal you. "Yes!" He will deliver you. "Yes!" He will set you free. "Yes!" He will supply your needs. You can count on God to keep his promises. He will never fail you."

It's the enemy's desire to use anything he can to get in your way and take your focus off of God. God spoke to me that this is the year of the open door and the manifestations of all that God promised us, but it seems like so many doors have been closed. I encourage you that if God promised it, believe it and it will come to pass. Stand firm! You can depend on the promises of God with absolute confidence that He will do what he says He will do. He freed you from your addictions, He delivered you from sin and evil, He provided for you even when you didn't know how you would make ends meet. He gave hope to the lost and hurting when you were on the verge of giving up. You overcame depression, healed your broken marriage, heal your body from all types of sickness and disease. God did it! He delivered you from fear and anxiety and now you walk in victory. If he did it before, He'll do it again. The same God back then is the same God right now.

Everything is working toward your blessings. So, stand firm in the Lord and on his promises. When we are weak, God promises to be our strength. God is always there to strengthen us, no matter what we may be going through. To be transparent, I know what it feels like not to have the strength to keep moving forward. Being a pastor does not exempt me from pain. But when I was at my weakest, that's when God was at his strongest. I'm encouraged in the word of God when he tells us, that we do not have to carry our burdens. He says to you today, "come unto me, you who are weary and heavy laden, and you will find rest for your souls". As we go through this journey called life the lord is always right there beside us. God promises He will never leave you. This is one promise I have stood on time and time again. The bible promises that no matter what we are facing, God will never leave us or forsake us. God has always been right there by my side.

Keep standing even in dire times. Keep trusting God. He will give you more than enough. He promises to prosper you. How can that be? No job, business closed down. This is when we remember the word of the Lord. Deuteronomy 30:9 The LORD your God will make you prosper abundantly in all the work of your hands (Christian Standard Bible). The LORD your God will make the labor of your hands abundantly successful. He didn't say your job or your business or your family or who you know will prosper you. He will use those things. But God said He will prosper you. Deuteronomy 8:18 NKJV, "Remember the LORD your God, for it is he who gives you power to get wealth. It is God's will that we prosper. Paul says in 3 JOHN 1:2 KJV: "Beloved, I wish above all things that thou mayest prosper and be in health, even as thy soul prospereth"."

God promises to hear your prayers. The bible tells us to Pray without ceasing. We must always pray and not faint. If there is ever a time to call on the name of Jesus, the time is now. God hears you. Nothing gets by God. He is sovereign over everything. This means he is in control. He knows what happening in the world. All we need to do is seek him. 2 Chronicles 7:14 KJV "If my people, which are called by my name, shall humble themselves, and pray, and seek my face, and turn from their wicked ways; then will I hear from heaven, and will forgive their sin, and will heal their land" Who are the my people" You and I collectively. We are the people of God. James 5:16 KJV tells us to "pray one for another, that ye may be healed. The effectual fervent prayer of a righteous man availeth much. If there is ever a time a pray, it is now". Pray people of God, Pray. And don't stop praying.

God promises to give you peace. In these difficult times, we need a peace of mind. Jesus left us with a gift of peace. So, don't be troubled or afraid. Jesus says in John 14:27 KJV "Peace I leave with you; my peace I give you. I do not give to you as the world gives. Do not let your hearts be troubled and do not be afraid. Philippians 4:7 KJV. And the peace of God, which passeth all understanding, shall keep your hearts and minds through Christ Jesus. We are told in verse 9, that during this storm, the God of peace will be with you.

God promised to always love you. The love of God is the constant and central message of the Bible. 1 John 4:9 KJV, "In this the love **of** God was made manifest among us, that God sent his only Son into the world, so that we might live through him. In this is love, not that we have loved God but that he loved us. John 15:13 KJV "Greater love has no one than this, that someone lay down his life for his friends". God's dealings with us are always out of grace. We are saved by grace, we are empowered for Christian service by grace, and we are kept by grace. God's love is always unmerited. John 3:16 KJV – For God so loved the world, that he gave his only begotten Son, that whosoever believeth in him should not perish, but have everlasting life. What love!!

Continue to stand firm on the Word of God. Do not waver or doubt what God says. God's word is sure. His word is truth. His word is everlasting.

——————— CHAPTER 4 ———————

Don't give up on Hope

Hold on to Hope. It is a confident expectation that God will do what he promised He will do. Although it has only been a few months into the new year, it is already filled with challenges and circumstances; leaving you to ask God, why does it seem each way I turn there is a storm and the year has just started for me? I want to encourage you not give up on Hope. In this season. God has directed me to share the message of Hope with everyone I come intact with. You should not waver in hope because it is rooted in the faithfulness of God. There should be moral certainty in it because the will and purpose of God are like iron, not chalk. Hope is not easily broken. Hope is a feeling of expectation and desire for a certain thing to happen. It is to desire with the expectation of obtainment or fulfillment. Hope is a desire for something good in the future. Psalm 37:4 Delight thyself also in the LORD: and he shall give thee the desires **of** thine heart" KJV.

Certainly, most would agree that these are challenging times in which we live. Yet, we are encouraged not to give up. 1 Corinthians 4: 8-9 KJV: We are troubled on every side, yet not distressed; we are perplexed, but not in despair; Persecuted, but not forsaken;

cast down, but not destroyed. No matter what comes our way, God has given us a way of escape. He will bring us out. The writer of Hebrews 4:16 KJV: tells us, "Let us therefore come boldly unto the throne of grace, that we may obtain mercy, and find grace to help in time of need". Take all of your cares to the Lord. He will work them out for you. Continue to trust in him with all your might as Proverbs 3:5 KJV directs us to "Lean not to your own understanding, but in all your ways, acknowledge him, and he will direct your paths.

Hope is a word of optimism and expectation that looks forward to a promising future, yet multitudes of people have lost their hope. Some feel hopeless about specific areas such as their marriage, children, health, finances, or job. For many hopelessness permeates their entire lives. They exist but have no hopes dreams, or goals. This is not the way God intends for us to live. He created us to live with purpose, working toward goals with a sense of anticipation for things to come. Romans 15:13 KJV, "Now may the God of hope fill you with all joy and peace in believing, that ye may abound in hope, through the power of the Holy Ghost" Romans 8:25 25 KJV tells us "But if we hope for that we see not, then do we with patience wait for it".

God does things that seem unusual to us in order for him to get us to where we need to be. God will use the very area that we claim can't be used or seem worthless and turn that into favor over our lives. It is okay to release our tears and ask questions to God when things seem unusual, but also in those moments, it also reminds us of our strength and will to know that God will keep his word and his promise. A word of knowledge to each of you is that in this season continue to be strong and continue to be steadfast in knowing who God has called you to be.

During difficult times, we must speak hope to ourselves, and speak it diligently and forcefully, or we will give way to a downcast and disquieted spirit within us. We have got to sing it. I just can't give up now, I've come to far from where I started from. God has brought me from a mighty long way. The best is yet to come. God knows, and He sees and is aware of everything that goes on in the life of His children. He knows your down sitting and he knows your uprising. Jesus knows all about you. You will make it and you will come out a winner.

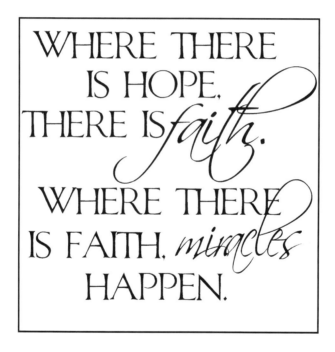

I have encountered those who feel that they are not even worthy to go to God in the time of need. No one is worthy, but Hebrews 4:16 KJV declares **"Let us** therefore come boldly unto the throne of grace, that we may obtain mercy, and find grace to help in time of need". Through God's grace and mercy, we can go to Him boldly any time we choose to. Before Jesus' death and resurrection, people couldn't just go to God when they wanted. During those times, when the high priest went to God behind the curtain of the Holy of Holies, it was in fear. If the high priest messed up, he died. But Jesus when he died for our sins, the curtain that separated the Holy of Holies was ripped from the top to the bottom. That curtain was meant to keep God in and us out. But now we have access to the throne of Grace. You can now go boldly to the throne of Grace to find help in the time of need.

May you be encouraged by knowing that God has His eye on you. God is faithful and He is going to fulfil all of His promises. Let us hold fast the confession of our hope, for He is faithful that promised. That he will withhold no good thing from us. Romans 8:28 KJV "And we know that for those who love God all things work together for good, for those who are called according to his purpose." It does not matter what you are going through don't give up on Hope. 2 Corinthians 3:12 NIV. "Since we have such a hope, we are very bold." Hope makes you bold. It will cause to you say, God will use these difficult times to cause a miracle to come forth in my life. Don't give up on hope.

CHAPTER 5

Moving from Your Comfort Zone

There are those who like to play it safe. We have the tendency to avoid trouble and difficulty. Have you ever missed out on a great opportunity because you played it safe? Think about it. Look back over your life and think about the things you could have done had it not been for playing it safe or for a lack of trusting God enough. If we want to obtain all that God has for us, we must defeat our desire to stay in our comfort zone. We must take on risks if we desire to move forward into the things God has promised us. We must defeat our desire to play it safe, in order to accomplish our goals and aspirations. It's time to move from your comfort zone into the Faith Zone. I have learned that I don't always have to see things, in order to trust God. I have learned to walk by faith and not by sight. I have walked out on faith in many areas in my life. And faith works.

There are some people who just don't believe that anything good can happen to you. They base this opinion on what they have seen in the past or what has happened to them in the past. All their lives, they have seen nothing or have been around nothing but negative things. People were always telling them what they can or cannot do. There are those who are always bringing up your past mistakes. If you focus on negative things enough, you begin to doubt if any good thing can ever happen to them. Stop listening to the negative and start believing the word of God, when He says you can do all things.

There are times when we allow problems to define who we are. We allow lack to determine our status in life. I don't have enough money. I don't have enough education. I am not smart enough. But I say these are just excuses for you to stay in your comfort zone. God wants you to know that there is a river of possibilities flowing to you. Jeremiah 29:11 KJV "For I know the thoughts that **I** think toward you, saith the LORD, thoughts of peace, and not of evil, to give **you** an expected end". Walking by faith allows God to release His plan for our lives. Yet, we allow problems to define who we are and where we are.

Stay away from negative folks. Those who question if you are making the right decision. Those whispering friends who secretly speak against you and the plan God has for you. There will always be someone who will not support you, and place doubt in your mind that will lead you to question if you heard from God. Do not let your emotions play games with your mind and with your faith. Your emotions will bring up everything negative in your mind to talk you out of moving forward. And before you know it instead of saying I can do this or that, you are now saying this is impossible for me to do. That's when we lean on the word of God and say to ourselves, over and over, I can do all things through Christ which strengthens me. There is nothing too hard for God. With God all things are possible. I am more than a conqueror.

I have learned some things about life and one thing in particular, among others is that life is an opportunity and we should benefit from it. Don't let life pass you by without ever realizing your dreams. There is no failure in God. There is no fear in God. I admonish you to live in the faith zone and not your comfort zone. Take risks and stop playing it safe. Playing it Safe can leave you unfulfilled, empty, un-rewarded and distant from God. Living by Faith means that we are victorious and over comers. To move into the faith zone, you must overcome the experiences of your past. When you are in the faith zone there are endless possibilities for your life. In addition, we must overcome the comforts of our now. John Maxwell, a Christian author said that it is a "Sad day when a person becomes absolutely satisfied with the life they're living, the thoughts they're thinking, the deeds they're doing – when there forever ceases to beat at the door of their soul a desire to do something greater for God."

So how does owning your own business, or going back to school, or learning to play that instrument causes you to do something great for God. It is simply because all that you do is by your faith in God. In our present, you develop a level of comfort which means that you grow accustomed to your lifestyle. You feel you have a secure place in your family situation, and you don't want to rock the boat. You feel secure in your current business or employment. You tell yourself I am too old to do anything different. By being comfortable in our present, we don't initiate anything new. We lose focus and we are not grounded. We become stagnant, at a standstill, and never moving forward. There are those who never move forward because of their insecurity or fear of the unknown. God will use our insecurities to build our dependence on Him. When we are uncertain about our future, we must lean on God, the one who knows our future in every detail. Do you know you can lean on God? He has promised to be with us every step of the way. The word of God said so. He promised to never to leave us or forsake us and to always be with us. And we must take him at this word.

Believe God that it your time and your season to break out of self-imposed limitations. Break out of negative thinking. Break out of insecurities. Break out of fears. Break out of past failures. Break out of where you came from and the limitations that were put on you. Break out of depression and hopelessness. Break out of a self-defeating mentality that says, "Nothing's ever going to change in my life." If you break out, then God's breakthrough can happen! You need to declare: "I'm not going to let these fears torment me. I'm not going to let failure dominate me. I'm not going to let my mistakes, or my past be lord over me. You can stir yourself to break out of whatever mind-set is holding you back".

The bible teaches us that that with God on your side, you're bigger than any problem. The question is whether or not you believe this enough to step out and allow God to use you. If you're just believing God for things you can do for yourself, you're limiting Him. Furthermore, if you think He'll never ask you to do things you can't do, think again. Jesus told one man to walk on water and another to come out of his grave—and they did. I can tell you from my own experience that when you find yourself amid things that are beyond your ability, that's when you know God is at work demonstrating His great power. Take what you have and put it into God's hands. The moment you make it available to Him, it will begin to grow. Growth begins when we leave our comfort zone. You can't stay the same and learn at the same time. Growth requires change. You have got to step out by faith. Don't be robbed of your greatest moments and memories.

Many people are so afraid of risk that they spend their entire lives in Egypt, the land of "not enough." God wants more for you! Get out of Egypt and into the promised land, the land of more than enough! It is by faith that you leave your comfort zone. It is by faith that you leave your safe zone. It is now time to move to the Faith zone, for Faith is required of you if you want to enjoy God's blessing to the fullest! Move now from your Comfort Zone.

---- **CHAPTER 6** ----

Quitting is Not an Option

Everybody has a bad day. Some have bad seasons. These are times when everything that can go wrong will and does go wrong. You and I know that life is heavy at times. Life throws us a ball that seems uncatchable. We must learn to lift our heads even if our hopes appear dashed. Even when it looks like things are not going to get any better, keep your head lifted up. Don't be rebellious to deny entry for the Lord and thereby forfeit blessings, because He is the One who is able to lift up your head.

There are times when I just felt like I could not go on. To be transparent, I've had my share of throw in the towel moments. There seem to be a battle going on in my mind, a relentless effort to take me off focus. That's when the Lord spoke to me from Psalm 24 in a very profound way. Keep your head lifted up. And I will come in for I am mighty in battle. For those who may be down and despondent and even depressed, God wants you to receive the same healing that I received from God in the word. "Lift up your heads, O ye gates; and be ye lift up, ye everlasting doors; and the King of glory shall come in (Psalms 24:7 KJV)."

Many times, we go through problems and circumstances alone,

smiling yet hurting. People around you expect you to be on task, polished, and proper all the time. But there are days when you are unsteady and unsure of yourself. This is when God reaches out without condemning you for your anxiety and doubts. I have been in this situation, not knowing which way to go, not knowing what to do, not knowing what to say. But I kept hearing God say to me, "Keep going, quitting is not an option".

It's at these times, that you open your hearts and minds and to give admission to the Lord to come in and take up residence. The one who is strong and mighty, the Lord, is ready to come in! Wow! Just imagine, how your life would be if you allowed the Lord to come into every situation and allow Him to solve every problem. But instead of waiting on the Lord for an answer, we quit. Instead we must settle at the feet of Jesus and wait for Him to direct our path.

Those of you who have been humiliated, mocked, persecuted, ignored, abandoned, and forgotten, receive today's word with open arms. Whatever you may be going through, there is a purpose for everything that happens in our life (good and bad). Sometimes they are simple things that seems to get us down. It is at those times that I have to keep reminding myself that I have the favor of God on my life. I have favor with God and man. There are things that sometimes have my head in the locks of my shoulders, not knowing which way to go in some cases. But God, did what he does best. He provided. He answered. Everything worked out for my good.

For those of you who may be going through trying times and you don't know what to do, and has not heard clear direction from God, do nothing, stand still, and wait on the Lord. And while you are waiting on the Lord, keep your head lifted up and allow the King of Glory to come in, He who is mighty and strong in battle. Some of your may have gone through sufferings, betrayals, pain, and losses. Do not lose hope. Some of you may have been rejected and who feel you are being treated poorly and unfairly. I know what that feels like. Don't give up. Don't take it to heart, for this is preparation ground to take you to higher levels. This is your testing season. So, pass the test. It's an open book test.

God wants to take you to but higher levels, so do not quit. You will be promoted in every area of your life. No one can demote you when God has decided to promote and exalt you! Trust God in all things. He will protect you and everything and everybody attached to you and you will come out victoriously. If you are going through pain and heartache from your spouse, your children, your family, your friends, your co-workers, your neighbors, your church, your school, …wherever…and however deep the pain may be, God wants to heal that pain so that you can keep your head lifted up. Psalm 3:3 KJV But you, LORD, are a shield around me, my glory, the One who lifts my head high. It is natural for the head to be bowed down in time of trouble. But God wants to lift your heads out of the locks of your shoulders. He wants to lift your head above all issues of life that may have you looking down and not up. Allow God to be the lifter of your head. He will bring you out of despair so that you are no longer bowing your head in misery and pain.

Since we belong to the Lord, there is nothing he will not do for us. God knows, God sees and God cares. The enemy wants us to believe that we are all alone and that nobody cares. That is a lie from the devil and there is no truth in him. God has His eye on you today. He knows where you are. He sees what you are going through. God knows everything because He is Omniscience. This means that He possesses total knowledge about everything that there is to know about you from your beginning to your end, and everything in between.

You are not alone. Psalm 139:7-10 KJV: Whiter Shall I go from thy spirit? Or wither shall I flee from thy presence. If I ascend up into heaven, thou art there: If I make my bed in hell, behold, thou art there. If I take the wings of the morning, and dwell in the uttermost parts of the sea: Even there shall thy hand lead me, and thy right hand shall hold me". God is never far from us and He is always with us. He observes everything that we do and watches everything that happens to us. He will not let any weapon formed against us to prosper. When I find myself in a difficult situation or not knowing which way to go, I whisper to myself "God you got this".

The writer of Hebrews 4:15 – 16 KJV tells us "that we have not a high priest which cannot be touched with the feeling of our infirmities; but was in all points tempted like as we are, yet without sin, let us therefore come boldly unto the throne of grace, that we may obtain mercy, and find grace to help in time of need. Family sometimes cannot help; friends sometimes cannot help. When there seems to be nobody that can help you, take it to Lord and you will find help in the time of need.

———— CHAPTER 7 ————

Wait Training

One of the important exhortations of the Bible is the call to "wait on the Lord." Even though God promises special blessing for waiting, waiting is one of the most difficult things to do. Why is it so hard? Because, we are so prone to take matters into our own hands, to follow our own devices when things do not happen when we want them to. Yet, over and over again we are told in the Scripture to "wait on the Lord." During the season of the COVID-19 virus, we have learned how to wait. The scripture tells us: But they that wait upon the LORD shall renew their strength; they shall mount up with wings as eagles; they shall run, and not be weary; and they shall walk, and not faint (Isaiah 40:31 **KJV**). Wait on the LORD: be of good courage, and he shall strengthen thine heart: wait, I say, on the LORD (Psalm 27:14 KJV). And let us not be weary in well doing for in due season we shall reap if we faint not (Galatians 6:9 KJV).

Waiting is difficult, but it is necessary especially if you are waiting on God to move in a particular situation. There is enough bad news to go around. But I have some good news. If we wait on the Lord to bring us out, we're going to make it. He's going to bring us through. Psalms 66 tells us that our God will bring us through to a wealthy place. I believe that there are those of us who will come out better than when we went into this crisis if we just trust in the Lord. In this season, it's not so much that we are waiting on God, but that God is waiting on us. He is waiting on us to be in the position to receive an answer from Him. Many times, we are out of position to even hear the voice of God. In this season of the coronavirus, many as asking how long. When will this be over? How much longer? And God is simply saying to us Wait. The word wait means to stay where one is or delay action until a particular time (Webster). In the Hebrew Scripture, wait means to bind together." It is that to which one's attention is bound. If there is ever a time for the church, the called-out body of believers to bind together it is now. As servants of Christ, it is imperative that our attention be bound to Him, not to religious activities or works but to God. Waiting means to stay in one place until another catches up: God is teaching us to wait on him. The blessings God has promised you will catch up to you if you just wait on the Lord.

Do not fret or be afraid, God has everything under control. You may be saying it seems like everything I were expecting has been put on hold. During this pandemic, every area of your lives has been touched: your health, your wealth, your jobs, your businesses, even the way we do ministry. Many of you have felt frustrated during this devastating time. I want you to know that you are not alone. There are others feeling the same way. What you are facing is not too big for God to solve. In an impatient world, it is essential for the believer to continue in prayer and wait on the Lord. He will answer. I've seen the word essential in this season more than I ever had. Essential businesses and non-essential business. Essential people and non-essential people. The word essential according to Webster means absolutely necessary; extremely important. One thing that

I know is essential, absolutely necessary, extremely important is that we trust God's timing. It is essential that we wait on God, for in due season, at the time He decides, His appointed time, we will reap if we faint not. If you learn to wait on God everything will turn out for your good.

The word of Lord in Isaiah 40:31 KJV should encourage us. "But they that wait upon the LORD shall renew their strength. The strength to stand. The strength to hold on. The strength to persevere. It is God who has given us this strength. When we get a little weak, God is always there to strengthen us no matter the situation. The Lord tells us that they that wait, "shall mount up with wings as eagles; they shall run, and not be weary; and they shall walk, and not faint". With wings of an eagle means that you will be able to soar over every set of circumstances in which you may find yourself. You will be able to soar above everything that wants to keep you down and despondent, that keeps you from obtaining all that God has for you. You are an eagle. Mount up with your wings and soar over the mountain. It's on the top of the mountain that you can see clearly. Being upon the mountain top is symbolic in life of overcoming your challenges. Not only will you be able to soar over the mountain, but you can speak to the mountain and demand that it be moved. The mountain is anything that gets in your way, that hinders you from receiving the blessings of the Lord. Don miss out because you refuse to wait.

For transparency sake, I don't like waiting either. I have found that waiting can be trying. I am no different from most of you. I don't like to wait in the doctor's office when I have an appointment. I don't like waiting in line at the grocery store. I don't like waiting in traffic. I just don't like to wait. But I'm learning to wait because waiting builds character and stamina. We must train ourselves not to give in or give up, but to remain steadfast.

Waiting involves the passing of time, which is itself a gift of God. The word wait carries the idea of confident expectation and hope. During this season of wait you might ask, what are we waiting for? During this season, someone who was straddling the fence, is now turning their lives completely over to God. During this season of wait, some parent's child is being saved, delivered, and set free. During this season of wait, someone is being delivered from addiction and bondage. During this season of wait, we are being healed in our spirits and our bodies. Oh yes, Lord we will wait. No matter how long it takes. No one will be able to take credit for this deliverance. Lord, you alone will get the glory out of this. And we will say God did it.

We will see that as we wait on God to move or to deliver, it helps us to gain a new level of trust in Him. God often lets us wait to help us build our faith. Waiting tests our resolve. Waiting tests our patience. God has a plan and a purpose for you in mind. God is training us to be able to receive what he has in store for us. So, don't miss out, simply because we refuse to wait. The time will come when the Body of Christ will tangibly see the manifestations of the promises of God. In this season, you are in "Wait Training!"

CHAPTER 8

The Benefits of Praise

First and foremost, God deserves to be praised and He alone is worthy to receive our praise. Praising God is the best thing you can do in a bad situation. Praising God makes every circumstance (good or bad) in our lives complete, essential, and worthwhile. The bible tells us, "In all things give thanks (1 Thessalonians 5:18

KJV). We are to give thanks in all circumstances. When Saul was out to kill David, he was so sure that God would deliver him that he wrote in Psalm 34 KJV, "I will bless the Lord at all times, His praise shall continually be in my mouth". At all times means God is to be praised in good as well in difficult times. David was saying, no matter what may be going on in my life, I will not stop praising the Lord. Praise should rise from all people for this is the will of God concerning you.

There are benefits to praising God. Our praise gives us an advantage over the enemy. God desires praise from His people. We are to give Him thanks in everything even through hardship. Praise is the clearest and most direct means of showing our total dependence on God. It shows our trust in Him in the midst of darkness. It confesses our allegiance and devotion to the One who was crucified for us and to whom we are eternally thankful. When Christians praise the Lord, it is the celebration of His goodness and grace. There are benefits to praising God and He wants you enjoy those benefits. The word benefit means something that provides happiness or does good for a person or thing (Webster). Even when you feel prone to give up use your weapon of praise to bring you through to the good things God has prepared for you. When you commit yourself to a life of praise and fellowship with Jesus, then and then only will you experience the fullness of God.

Praise puts our focus on God, and not on our problems. Praise establishes our faith. The greater we see our God; the smaller we see our problems. Praise elevates our emotions. Worry, fear, and doubt cannot survive in an atmosphere of praise. Praise causes God to move on our behalf. God inhabits the atmosphere of praise. Praising God is useful and favorable for us. By praising God, we are reminded of the greatness of God! His power and presence in our lives is reinforced in our understanding. If we want to see a clear manifestation of God's blessings and grace, all we need to do is to praise Him with all our heart, our mind, and our soul. Praise helps us complete God's primary purpose for creating us, which is to glorify Him.

In II Chronicles 20: 1 – 27 KJV, we are told that the armies of the Moabites, Ammonites, and others had declared war on King Jehoshaphat. The word came to Jehoshaphat that "A vast army is marching against you". And just like King Jehoshaphat received bad news, we from time to time receive news that has devastated us. Some have received news about the loss of a loved one; others have received news that their children have been arrested; and some have received news of being diagnosed with cancer or some other disease. You may receive news that your homes were being foreclosed or your automobiles are being repossessed. The question is, what do you do when you receive bad news? The bible says that King Jehoshaphat was terrified by the news he received. But instead of acting on his fears, he sought the Lord for guidance. The bible declares that Jehoshaphat stood before the people where he prayed and called on the Lord. He prayed reminding God that He had ran off their enemy from the land and had given it to the Israelites for an in heritance. Jehoshaphat prayed," God you told us that if we call upon you would come and see about us". Sometimes we must remind God of his promises. In fact, we are told to "Put the Lord in remembrance of His promises and keep not silence" (Isaiah 62:6 KJV). God invites you to remind him of his promises.

While Jehoshaphat was yet praying and seeking God, the Spirit of the Lord came upon one of the men in the midst who was moved to speak. The prophet of God said, "Listen, all you people of Judah and Jerusalem! Listen, King Jehoshaphat! This is what the

Lord says: Do not be afraid! Don't be discouraged by this mighty army, for the battle is not yours, but God's. In this battle you will not have to fight. When you go out, take you position, be still and see the salvation of the Lord. He is with you. Do not be afraid or discouraged". The Lord is telling us the same today. Don't fret or worry because of the Corona virus, God will bring us out. In the end we will win.

And when Jehoshaphat had consulted with the people, he appointed singers unto the LORD, and that should praise the beauty of holiness, as they went out before the army, and to say, "Praise the LORD; for his mercy endures forever". When trouble comes into your life, take a praise break. And as soon as they began to sing and to shout praises, GOD set ambushes against their enemies. The praises of the people of God, confused their enemies, and they began to kill each other off. When Judah took a look over in the valley, they found dead bodies and not a living soul among them. And the bible says that when Jehoshaphat and his people came to take away the spoil of them, they found among them in abundance both riches with the dead bodies, and precious jewels, which they stripped off for themselves, more than they could carry away: and they were three days in gathering of the spoil, it was so much. There are benefits to praising God. There was so much, it took them three days to cart it away! GOD had given them joyful relief from their enemies!

The enemy doesn't know what to do with you who refuses to give up. Keep praising God through the pain to your victory. Praise is a powerful part of our walk with God. Make a point to give God praise in all situations. Paul tells us in 1 Thessalonians 5:18 KJV - "In everything give thanks for this is the will of God in Christ Jesus concerning you" I encourage you to praise God for what seems like the simplest of things. Praise God even when the enemy seems to have the upper hand. Choose Praise as your weapon of choice against your enemy. If it worked for Jehoshaphat and the people of Judah, how much more will your praise work for you during turbulent times. Praise honors God's presence. It also honors God's greatness when we are able to magnify God and focus on his goodness in spite of our personal challenges. God inhabits the praises of his people. There are benefits to praising God. Let everything that has breath, praise the Lord. Amen!

Bibliography

Strong, James. *Strong Exhaustive Concordance of the Bible*. Hendrickson Publishers Marketing, LLC. Peabody MA. 2007.

The Essential Evangelical Parallel Bible. Updated Edition: New King James Version, English Standard Version, New Living Translation, The Message. Oxford University Press, Inc. New York, NY. 2004.

The Merriam-Webster Dictionary. https://www.merriam-webster.com retrieved April 21 2020.

About the Book

There are times when many feels like they just could not take another day of sorrow; times when some wanted to throw in the towel. Those who felt like all hope was gone. The chapters of this Book are meant to encourage you to keep pushing forward. and to just hold on to the promises of God. There is help for you during the most challenging times of one's life. I believe that this book will revive you and get you back to your purpose. It is the desire of this book to inspire you to move forward in life and to hold on to hope. Hope is a feeling of expectation of obtainment or fulfillment. Hope is a desire for something good in the future. This book will bring you or someone you know who feel overwhelmed and who are struggling in life both healing and wholeness. This book encourages you to stay hopeful in the midst of doubt. As you read this book, allow God to guide you through the plans he has for you. Plans for good and not for disaster, to give you a future and a hope. Your help is on the way!

About the Author

Bishop Hattie Dancil-Small is a native of North Carolina. She has been ministering the word of God for thirty-five years. For the past 16 years she has served as Senior Pastor of Kingdom Harvest Outreach Ministry Inc. which she found. Bishop Small currently lives in St. Petersburg, FL. She is known as the encourager. It is her desire to give support, confidence, and hope to everyone she meets regardless of their life experiences, talents, physical ability, or role—they have a purpose and a destiny. What matters the most is that they remain faithful.

Bishop Small is a graduate of St. Petersburg College and Eckerd College and has both an Associate and Bachelor's Degree in Business Management, respectively. She holds a Master's in Education from St. Leo University. She has an Associate and

Bachelor's degree in Theology from Faith Theological Seminary & Christian College, Tampa, Florida and is currently working toward a Doctorate in Theology. Bishop Small was confirmed a Bishop in July 2018 under the Sounds of Praise Pentecostal Fellowship Ministry, Worldwide under the leadership of Apostle Allen H. Simmons. Bishop Dancil has worked in several positions in the insurance industry for almost 30 years. For the last 12 years, she was a reading teacher in both middle and high schools.

After the death of her husband and the loss of her job in 2003, Bishop Small found herself in a state of brokenness, but instead of giving up, she set herself to seek the Lord. After much prayer, she began an outreach ministry which has evolved into a full-time ministry. She continues to be fueled by inspiration from Jesus Christ and the driving desire to fulfill the Lord's will for her life, and a dedication for winning souls for the Kingdom.

Her favorite saying is, "And We Shall Say God Did It".

Printed in the United States
By Bookmasters